The Faith of Fragile Things

The Faith of Fragile Things

Collected Poems by

Kevin Shyne

Cover design by Shay Culligan
Cover illustration by Mary C. Shyne, daughter of the author

ISBN: 978-1-63980-226-5

Kelsay Books
502 South 1040 East, A-119
American Fork, Utah 84003
Kelsaybooks.com

This collection is dedicated to my friend and teacher, Nancy Friedlander, in whose high school English class, poetry came alive.

Acknowledgments

After Hours: "The Illustrated Daughter"

The Avocet: "The Faith of Fragile Things," "The Jigsaw Forest," "Mulberry Tree"

Better Than Starbucks: "Letter to the Occupant"

The Blue Unicorn: "Before Her Next Admission"

Clementine Unbound: "How Hard She Tries," "The Minuet Before Goodbye," "Parked in the Sixties," "The Valentine"

The Grey Sparrow Journal: "Our Lady Burning"

The Lyric: "The Bookmark," "The Sounds of Souls We Love"

Poetry Breakfast: "Before the Cleaners Come," "Logan's Bath," "Not on a Leash," "The Souvenir," "Weekend Update"

Poetry Porch: "Mastering the Music"

The Road Not Taken: "Burning Leaves," "Lost Keys"

Third Wednesday: "Is This How Meeting God Will Be?"

Vox Poetica: "Wash on Gentle"

I would also like to acknowledge poet and novelist Marydale Stewart, without whose encouragement and advice this book would not have been possible.

Contents

Four: *Good as grass, a gentle state of mind*

Five: *Forgive me if your name wriggles free*

Six: *Follow the sound of singing*

One:
Nothing separates my soul from theirs

The Illustrated Daughter

My daughter's first tattoo—
an e. e. cummings line
inked in cursive script
across her shoulder blade—
set off alarms, but she was 21.
I held my tongue, relieved at least
that her disfigurement
was poetic as it was discreet.

I should have known
the first foretold
a rising tide of ink
no father could resist
until when fully dressed
her colors spilled out unconfined
at neckline, ankles, nape, and wrist.

Here, the badge of her career,
a nurse's face in reds and blues.
There, in tribute to grandmothers' love
a lighthouse beams across a thigh
a needle glides upon the other.
Her forearm and her husband's
share a sleeve,
colorized indelibly
unfrayed by daily wear.

In time, I looked upon her marks
half-bemused, not thinking
I would ever comprehend
until a rolled-up sleeve revealed
the image of a plumed quill pen
the nib dipped in a bottle
embellished with her sister's name:
a writer and cartoon creator,

an honored guest within
a sea of stories crashing
on a coast of ink and skin.

As if an inner tide had turned,
the whole that had begun
with poetry extended by
the emblems of her heart
became a gallery adorned
with living works of art.
At last, all reservation put to rest
I saw unblinded by my fears
her tattoos form a whirling arabesque
so beautiful it stained my face with tears.

The Minuet Before Goodbye

On Sunday afternoon
my daughter calls me back
while making lunches,
saving every penny
for treks she takes
to destinations off the grid.
Clinking in the background
is her butter knife, the clapper
in a bell of mayonnaise
nine hundred miles away.

Her voice, bejeweled
by her originality,
rolls through me in a rising tide.
I stream like seaweed in her current.
Our catch-up conversation
crests on words
more said than understood.

You have her eyes . . .
the last time you were here . . .
the years go flying by.

On another day, her hand in mine,
our faces close,
her bucket full of shells,
she held one to my ear.
I said, *Hello, is this the ocean?*

But now she has to go.
Friends are waiting at the door.
She says goodbye,
not wanting me to hear
their rollicking commotion.
The phone held to my ear,
I strain to hear the ocean.

Mastering the Music

Laura, age 13, first chair violin,
seats her instrument beneath her chin.
Suspended on a string, a girl
swings above a woman's world.

She sweeps her bow across the strings
to liberate arpeggios.
Her tremulous vibratos make
the dotted half and whole notes quake.
Her nimble fingers find and linger on
adagios that Mozart left behind.

She takes the lead and soars
beyond the realm of scale and metronome
as if she hears an overture
of emotions hers and hers alone.
Never has she felt so sure
of bowmanship and fingercraft.
This brave new world is vast.
Across the universe she flies, unafraid
of mastering the music as she is played.

At Laura's age has anybody ever known
the difference between flight and falling like a stone?
She could be plummeting. No one would know,
except a man in the second row.
He would rush the stage, cause a scene, but no . . .
how hard to have a daughter, age 13, and let her go.

All Things Beautiful in Their Time

Laura on a bicycle,
I on foot beside
my five-year-old shadow
out of training wheels
keeping up, a mile to go
in rhythm with my stride.
Touched by her faithful
two-wheeled flight,
I put our ramble into words,
a journal entry dated 1991.

More than twenty years slid by
before I paused to greet
the day my journal saved
as if this page awaited me,
like an old friend long since
moved away but stopping by
while in the neighborhood.

Abashed, I reread the lines.
For all that I remembered
about that summer day
it might have never been
except for evidence
in my own hand
on a journal page.

But graciously imagination
patched the unremembered gaps.
I pictured Laura then
on a trail so often run
I once knew every turn and rise.

As if peering through a window
that brings the past in sight,
I lingered on our page
in thanks for afterglow
of our recovered light.

The Christmas Truce

On Christmas Eve, 1914
five months into World War I
soldiers on both sides set down their guns.
They ventured into no man's land
to join in caroling with men they'd come to kill.

A century since then I lie in bed awake,
my wife beside me sound asleep.
Our daughters home from college
went to bed an hour ago.
I listened to them tapping on their keyboards,
bursts of keystrokes like popcorn popping
until the last few kernels sputtered out.

On every other night, anxieties I bring to bed
feast upon my wakefulness. A snap
sounds in the dark, as if a boot
had stepped upon a twig.
I crouch, not wanting to be crept up on.
I wrestle thoughts of young men's careless cruelty,
leaving dark tattoos upon my daughters' innocence.
I shift an arm to touch my wife—not to wake her
but to know she's there. I wonder though
will I be left behind by workshops and her art
deferred for years by patient motherhood?

My nighttime enemies, knowing of the absences
of daughters more often gone than home
or wife away on weekends with her friends,
have found new hand and footholds
to scale my peace of mind.

Prayer holds anxieties at bay
yet even as I pray their legions rumble,
massing for a fresh attack.

Tonight for once my smoking battlefield is still.
I shake hands with my fears.
Our bloody feud will wait
as long as it takes to wed a wife,
to make a home and welcome friends,
to make mistakes and learn to love
exactly who we are.

As long as it takes to agonize in labor twice
to sing our daughters off to sleep
to teach them how to ride their bikes
to learn to wait until they want to talk
to believe after years of pushing us away,
they'll come home.

No matter what tomorrow brings,
my world is safe tonight.
So come out from your trenches, monsters,
dance in your bloody boots, arm in arm with me
in the mud of our Christmas Truce.

Logan's Bath

Logan, 14 months, stands beside his mother
on her knees. Swishing with her hand,
she tests the water in the tub,
fiddles with the faucet, and finds the perfect mix.

Leaning in, belly pressed to porcelain,
entranced by water gushing from the spout,
Logan slaps above the waterline in pure delight.
His perfect fingers break the silver skin,
dipping deeper in, he sees his submerged arms
refracted to the right.
He makes a fist and laughs
discovering that water can't be squished
but it will bend the light.

How little does he comprehend
of optical illusions
of volume that his hand displaces
of pipes and drains
of stains dissolved in aqueous solution
of rites of absolution
of faith in God's reunion when we rise
of immersion in the meanings
water comes to symbolize?

My daughter lifts him up and in.
He splashes, kicks, his eyes go wide.
He has no words to analyze or name
this wondrous stuff.
His laughter is enough.

Standing in the open door
I watch and realize
I'd give the world to see the water gush
through Logan's eyes.

Modern Mother

Amid routines and requisites,
imperatives, necessities,
the sundry caveats of modern motherhood,
before the seatbelts click
before the paying, sorting, washing, drying,
parking, shopping, zipping, tying,
before the trusting eyes
of backseat passengers
beheld in her rear view,
she takes creation by the wheel
her hands at 10 and 2.

Letter to the Occupant

Not long ago I was a home
but now I'm property,
a listing in the classifieds:
three BRs, two Bs.

You crossed my threshold man and wife
then brought your newborns home to me.
How far they've come since they first crossed
my hardwood floors on hands and knees.

You framed their pictures, K through 12,
to lavish love upon.
I lived to be the wall
you hung their pictures on.

I lay awake with you one night
the moon upon my window sills
your hand upon your spouse's side
your children sleeping steps away.
When I was less and less their home
they'd visit for the holidays.

Arriving late, too late you hoped
to plan an evening out,
they joined you in a game of cards
then off to bed to settle in
to my familiar company.

I listened as you kept your watch,
your loved ones safe, secure and near
then took your place so you might sleep
beyond the reach of woe or fear.
Don't think you kept me from my rest.

Your vigil honored me.
My joists and rafters settled in
and creaked contentedly.

Then came the sign I'd seen before
in front of former neighbors' yards
as if to say our neighborhood
were built with balanced playing cards.
I never thought you would impale
the lawn you tended lovingly
and hang me up for rent or sale
on a post for all to see.

Then I watched you pack your things
and check for items left behind.
The etching on my sidewalk stays
to mark the place your children signed
their monograms on wet concrete.
I won't forget how proud I stood
with their initials at my feet.

I understand your kids are grown,
my stairs are tough on aging knees.
After all that we've been through
you have my sympathies.

Eventually I'll dwell in peace
but not today, I can't.
As you give my keys away
indulge me in a farewell rant
and promise me you'll file these words
with your closing documents
to be retained for future use
by the current occupants.

The Plastic Fighter Jet

One Christmas, there was a boy
who begged for that year's must-have toy:
the cockpit of a plastic fighter jet
for heroes bound for glory
not unlike Ralphie Parker,
the teller of *The Christmas Story.*

There's nothing that I've ached for more
since then except a story like his,
a fable filled with my illusions
come to life for all to see
the foolishness of being tricked
by flying things seen on TV.

For isn't it true, as Ralphie learned
that getting the wanted thing—
the hoping, the having, the disillusion—
is how you get what you really want
like a family Christmas dinner
at a Chinese restaurant.

Before Her Next Admission

When my grown child
gets too much on track
early birding, eating less
speeding up and working up a sweat,
when she seems as sharp and centered
as her flawless silhouette
saying all the right words
about what it takes to heal,
then my foot rides on the brakes
that aren't there. My hands reach for
the missing steering wheel.

I should be glad for her,
rejoicing in her alteration.
I want to trust in medicine,
believe that therapy will take
that this time will be different,
a turnaround, not running off,
missing pieces trailing in her wake.

On the tightrope of a mirror
her image seems to shake.
Did she teeter or did I?
Do I hinder her recovery
anticipating slips before
she has a chance to try.

Then I know it's time to take a breath,
give her space, worry less, and pray
make peace with mental illness,
be thankful that she's here today.

How Hard She Tries

Say it was her command.
My daughter, age eleven,
stared me down
until I said the words,
I love myself.

But obedience was not enough.
She drilled me with her eye.
Now with feeling, she persisted
as if to say
If you can't why should I?

Softening her stare,
she granted me a night's reprieve
attentive as I tucked her in
kissed her cheek,
and left the door an inch ajar.
In the hall I tried again.
I love myself
spoken in a voice I barely recognized.
Much easier to say and mean
I love you to a child like this
but turn the words back on ourselves
we choke on undeservingness.

Tomorrow night I'll try again
as much for her sake as for mine.
One day, when I am but a face
watching from a picture frame
hanging on a daughter's wall
she'll catch me eyeing
her surrender and wonder
what happened to her spine.

Then she will remember,
besieged by her own children's eyes
how easily the words
I love myself
once came to her
and now how hard she tries.

The Valentine

Beside me in my nursing home
you unfold a yellow page
and read the little poem
I wrote for you before old age
had robbed us of familiar ground.

Let our day be put away,
lost, then one day found
between the pages of a favorite book,
thick and leather-bound.

You read each line and wait
in hopes that I might recognize
this ancient valentine.
The nurse stops by. She says it's late.
You see a flicker in my eyes.

Could it be a sign
that proves at least I've heard?
It's as if I said in spoken words
as my vital signs were noted,
"That's beautiful my dear. Who wrote it?"

Seaside Park, New Jersey

My father, frail but bold,
advances on the boardwalk
with studied steps
as if to prove his legs
could pass a walking test.
Each time he stops, I unfold
a lightweight chair for him to rest.

Sand dunes hide the beach,
but not the sky
not the wheeling gulls
not the ocean's roar
not the kites on arcing strings.
What better place
for him to soar
among the real and paper wings?

Uplifted by an ancient tide
beside a sandy shore
thankful for his tardy pace
I pause to memorize
his windburned face
his drowsing eyes
his salty snore.

Not on a Leash

Grief cannot be trained to sit and stay
or walk beside you on a leash.
When a door is left ajar, it dashes out
to lead you on a game of hide and seek.

Grief won't be groomed with comb or brush.
It sheds wherever fur is wanted least.
You'll find it napping on your favorite chair
not budging when you try to take the seat.

Grief will not retrieve a far-flung stick
or give you back the toy between its teeth
but it will fetch forgotten days
and drop them squarely at your feet.

Grief will stray but in the end
it scratches at your door, weary, worn, and weak,
begging to be taken in, lifted up,
allowed to rest in peace.

Having hollowed out your heart,
grief nestles in, to heal,
to be made whole, and sleep.

The Sounds of Souls We Love

From an upper room, I hear their muffled noises:
footsteps, the clattering of pots and pans, the stirring
of a spoon, a cough, the splash of running water,
unnoticed until someone turns it off.

Sick in bed, I imagine busy souls below:
the details of their hands and faces,
their shape and size, the way they hold their arms
in gestures that appear before my eyes.

Nothing separates my soul from theirs: no cares,
no thoughts of things I should have said or done
to interfere with my perceiving. The thickets
of my busy mind have opened on a clearing.

I have come to healing night: to where
I see by ear more clearly than by sight.
With scattered stars above, the night and I are one
united by the sounds of souls we love.

Two:
A lion-hearted army roams the woods

The Death of Chivalry

A lion-hearted army roams the woods
in heraldry of old.
The maples don their coat of arms—
crimson leaf on field of gold.
Orange is the oak's escutcheon.
The ash in purple raves.
They would the warmth of summer save,
led to war by generals
on a quest a month too far.

The cadence of October beats
and stirs the blood of new recruits
even as the sap retreats
to safety in the roots.
Silently the conifers
observe the army's might,
whose regiments deride the birds
too cowardly to stay and fight.

And so, the signs of danger missed
every bough and blade enlists
from undergrowth to canopy
upon a glorious crusade
to meet their mortal enemy
without regret and unafraid.

Then comes the wind with fang and claw.
Offended by the golds and reds,
he rips the canopy to shreds
and strips the understory raw.
Next comes rain, who six months ago
helped the forest bud and grow.

Now she turns her silver keys
unlocking stubborn leaf from limb.
The trees are by her treacheries
completely taken in.

The leaves fall back in disarray.
The brave close ranks to hold their ground
only to be smashed away
when winter hammers down.
In the end the slaughtered heaps
lie bleeding at their generals' feet
whose creaking limbs entreat,
pleading to be left in peace
without a flag to wave a truce,
not that it would be of use
or honored in the least.

There are no neutral parties
on winter's killing field.
Without unbloodied enemies
nor holdouts yet to yield,
the wind comes after me.

Laughing as he swings his lash,
he would flay my flesh from bone,
or at very least, hurl a vicious blast
and send me limping home
with my sack of metaphors and well-chosen words.
He would take possession of the woods
alone and unobserved.

The Jigsaw Forest

I walk the fallen woods alone
the branches bared above my head
a jigsaw forest at my feet.

How can the forest rest
with its foliage in disarray
as if abandoned by summer guests
hurrying to get away?
They leave their puzzle strewn about
denying having seen the box
with a pictured woods on top.

But what the guests have left behind
will be made right in four month's time
by patient hands of rain and snow.
Each piece among a trillion they will turn
and place where it alone will go.
They form a finished forest
from pieces joined in twos and threes.
By March, for all their trouble,
the blossoms and the canopy
will be an uncompleted puzzle
until when May begins
a mad green rush will fill it in.

The rain and snow would stare in disbelief
were my oafish hands of flesh and bone
to lay a single piece.
Still it comforts me to walk the woods alone
imagining I've found an edge or corner leaf.

Mulberry Tree

I dreamed I was a tree, but not an elm
casting shade across a boulevard,
nor a spruce or fir to frame a winter scene.
I didn't dream myself a maple
dripping watercolor on a forest floor,
neither chestnut, oak or dappled sycamore.

No, I was merely mulberry,
back-alley tree, frowned upon,
braiding golden fingers into chain link fences
and sneaking uninvited into privet hedges.

Give me a year in any ground
beyond a mower's reach
I'll root myself too deep for pulling out by hand.
A mattock or a shovel would do
for another year or so
but let me go for four or five,
you'll need a chainsaw and a crew.

Full grown, I top the ranks of nuisance trees.
My fibrous branches make a poor excuse
for firewood or planks.
My roots will crack your neighbor's water main.
Turn around, I'll be straining at your power lines.
All summer, sidewalks wear my berries
like a bad complexion.
Walk the lawn below my musky shade,
you'll track out purple everywhere you go.

And yet, your children climb
my low-forked trunk with ease.
My spreading boughs can be a row of bleacher seats,
my overhanging limbs a stairway
to a rooftop envied from below.

My berries bring the birds:
thrushes, robins, thrashers, orioles,
a flock of flaming drunks attracted to an open bottle,
beating wings and tails against my glossy green.

Awake, I live by plans and promises
hiding who I am among the better trees,
but in my deepest sleep I am mulberry,
not to beauty born. Beauty comes to me.

The Faith of Fragile Things

The maple seeds of May
unfasten from their branches.
How slight their chances
of taking root someday,
much less rising up a tree.

For a moment free
revolving paper wings
depart the canopy
to sail off spiraling
toward immortality.

Who could improve
these maple fingerlings?
Before the evidence is gone
let us reflect upon
the faith of fragile things.

Bearing precious freight,
how well they navigate
their taste of liberty
centered by the weight
of possibility.

Stunned

The thunk that caught my ear
led me to fear the worst:
a clump of plumage
thwarted by a door of sliding glass.

No creature free to fly
should lie the way it lay:
breast down, spread-eagled,
head folded in. The birder
in me recognized
a downy woodpecker:
a checkerboard of black and white
across its grounded wings,
a scarlet patch, the swatch
upon its head no field guide
color-plate could match.

Dead or only stunned I couldn't tell
but watched and agonized.
Should I step outside for pity's sake?
The crisis seemed to have intensified
the loveliness at stake.

Coming closer,
I saw a blink, a shake,
a tremble in its tail
when all at once
a feathered bolt shot up,
one moment still,
the next a pair of beating wings
alighting on a branch
if not to sing at least
to verify the sky
was put back in one piece.

Resilient bird, undaunted
by an obstacle of glass,
but no more stunned than I
to realize a miracle
had come to pass.

Burning Leaves

The air came crackling
underfoot at dawn
driving me outdoors to see
the immolation of the trees.
I caught my breath,
blown away and yet discerning
violence and savage voices.
Good air for burning.

I joined my neighbor, blistering
our hands in a fit of raking,
but our trouble was as nothing
to the birds' awaking. They gathered,
sparked, flamed out, arced
in a migratory churning,
kindling a forest fire in flight.
Good air for burning.

The birds were flying embers
but their frenzy was as nothing to the leaves,
a mob of hooligans, wrecking the arena
jumping rails to riot in the field,
reckless, unrefereed,
trampled by October's turning
while geese in wedges split the sky.
Good air for burning.

Our leaf pile writhed
into a curbside dragon's head
but its roaring was as nothing to the turmoil in the air
stripping men of words, leaving us to gorge
the fire-breathing beast and flash each other signs
as men will do concerning
a love, a leap, a season lost.
Good air for burning.

Three:
I remembered how to genuflect

The Souvenir

At Connemara Marble
on tour in Ireland
you bought a rosary
handmade from polished stones
sea green, black veins
the quarry's stock-in-trade
connected by a sturdy chain,
as if for hands too stiff
to finger through
more closely spaced decades.

In 30 years of marriage,
I've never seen you pray a rosary
looped about your hands
devoutly kissed
pressed palm to palm in prayer
your promises to God
sealed by a dangling crucifix.

I kept my peace, stood aside,
observing as you paid,
a witness to your holy whim,
a souvenir to venerate
or something bought for buying's sake,
a bauble in disguise of piety
too lovely to resist.

On either score
some grace may come of it.
What else about your intercourse
with heaven have I missed?
What innocence in jeopardy
or weary refugee
do your secret prayers protect?

Later, in the ruins of an ancient church
I remembered how to genuflect.

Before the Cleaners Come

I clear the kitchen counters,
empty the dish-drying rack,
tuck sponge and brush below the sink,
hook broom behind the closet door.

The kitchen, dining room, and hall are mine,
as we agreed some time ago
dividing up domestic chores.
I check the other rooms
for anything of mine not put away.
The rest is yours.

The night before the cleaners come—
every other week lest housework
be a cause for us to disagree—
your rooms are spread
with cross-stitch patterns,
skeins of floss and pages torn
from magazines.
Your finished needlework,
rolled in paper towel tubes,
crowds the coffee table.
Tote bags hang from backs of chairs.
Scissors, tape and wrapping paper
lie where they have lain
since your niece's baby shower.
CDs still wrapped in cellophane
mingle with the paperbacks
in need of bookshelf space.
They'll have to wait. For every book
you read, two others take its place.
Bulging shopping bags reveal
the contours of your latest purchase.
The sales receipts roost here and there
as if our house were visited by paper birds,
making nests on every horizontal surface.

Later on tonight,
I hear your pre-clean frenzy
while reading by myself in bed,
or getting up to offer unrequested help
with tasks you're storming through.
I hold my tongue, never having found a way
to speak and not become the echo of your father.
Besides, no matter what I said
you wouldn't start until the night before
turning something simple
if done in daily increments
into something furious.

Still I'm curious.
Could we avert the rush
before the cleaners come . . .
and still be us?

The Flannel Man

I guard our house in stocking feet
a softly stepping flannel man
amid the whirring
of the bathroom fan
the furnace rumble
the freezer's hum
their sounds as close to nourishment
as flavors on my tongue.

On my watch
each room becomes
an instrument
plucked randomly
as if our house were practicing
its scales while you are gone.

Now I must wait
unspeak your name
wear my flannels inside out
until your comfort comes and I
surrender to your sweet demands
your warmth against my arms
against your face against my hands.

The Bookmark

I know a world not orbiting the sun,
a satellite my restless mind has spun.
Its force of gravity is handmade from
the pages turned by fingertip and thumb.

Inhabiting this world two lovers rage,
thwarted by an ordinary bookmark
no character could breach or understand.
The cast of two, unbearably delayed,
is poised to leave the safety of the dark.
About to leap, they teeter hand in hand
a word away from casting off the curse
of fearing who would hurt the other first.
Disguises dropped and rumpled at their feet,
they redden in a forest fire's heat
at last beside the lover each is meant
to find before their story line is spent
nothing left between them but a page unturned.

I left their world and to your arms I fled,
a bookmark wedged as far as I had read.
You held my place, faithful, unconcerned.
It's late my dear, you sighed. *Now come to bed.*

Euclid's Love Song

Love is a ray.
Its origin is known,
the center of a ring of ripples
from a pebble thrown.

The infinite is puzzling
disguised as line or ray.
If one defeats our sense of length
along an endless graph
what are we to make of infinity by half?

From a point in space and time
loves goes on forever
providing proof that flesh and bone
are mingled with divinity
headed to infinity
on our journey home.

Some might prefer to dwell
in then and now
and realms of yet to be.
As for me, I'll take forever
cut asunder
beginning in the heart
and going where the Gods can only wonder.

Our Lady Burning

In a faded photograph
of Paris, my younger self
a child of God
poses with the world's beloved crone
dwarfed by Notre Dame's façade
her ancient portals crowned
by gospels told in stone.

You were in nursing school
as unaware of me as I of you
my future bride.
Who'd have known
the day our lady burned
we'd suffer side by side?

We watched in horror,
the present burning up our past
as if the spire that marriage built
wobbled, tilted, crashed,

as if our lady wept
for thousand-year-old oak
her shoulders shrouded by
a raveled shawl of smoke,

as if her tears
could keep the fire
from blackening our wedding photograph
our younger faces beaming
in the unburned half.

My Funny Valentine

There you are
self-dramatizing
misinformed
up on your high horse
neighing at the world.

I should hide
be gone for good
or ball up all the times
I've let things pass
and hurl them back at you
but not before
I've understood the reason
you make me feel alive.

How could I run away
from the person in whose eyes I see
reflections of the good and wise in me?

Exasperating you
and what's worse
you're worth the trouble
hovering above
a man made gullible
enough to love
and feel lovable.

Making Love

What is love made of?
Not the cards in our wallets
not the color of our skins
not the accent of our voices
not the genes of common kin
but
arriving at the same time, coincidentally
being caught off guard, gently
a certain tone of voice
no one else may know
not holding on or off or back
but strangers letting go.

Matrimonial Erosion

Our anniversaries mean more
when years as man and wife outnumber
years that came before.
They say let no man put asunder
those whom God has joined.
Still, I wonder, was it divinity or weather
that bound our lives together?

Wedding vows unite two states
bringing down the gates and fences.
The crossing zones, once marked with yellow stripes,
are beautified with flower beds and benches.
A nationality in common,
back and forth the spouses go
forging bonds that love
and common property bestow.

If weddings blur a boundary
geography more slowly changes.
Between a bridegroom and a bride
there is a watershed divide.
The ridges of their mountain ranges
separate the snow and rain.
To different seas their rivers drain.

But wind and water have their way,
wearing mountains into hills
a grain of sand a day.
Canyons into valleys spread,
valleys into plains.
Given time their rough terrain
is leveled to their riverbeds.

Our anniversary more times repeated
than years that passed before we met,
we celebrate at last our wedding's work completed
by every drop of rain and flake of snow.
Blessed by matrimonial erosion
our lives unseparated flow
into a single ocean.

Two Runners

Two runners threaded through
a maple grove to where
the woods gave way
to a clearing
on Fairhaven Bay.
You waded in, as did I.
Your features mirrored on reflected sky
as if the day had been designed
for leaving loneliness behind.

When I recall your voice,
your eyes and face,
the place a broken runner's emptiness
was left upon a pebbled shore,
then the flood of tenderness
a memory can bring
wells up and takes my breath away
circled by a wooded ring around a silver bay.

The runner that you were is gone.
I am a man marooned no more.
Our lives went on, I found my way,
a loving wife, a good career,
lovely daughters I adore.
From your Christmas cards I know
you too have made a life, married well,
count your blessings and are counted so.

Yet I recall my fragile years.
Your kindness carried men like me.
I wonder now how many
of the lonely ones you saved

ever had a chance to say
how much your haven meant
or how the memory would stay
like a vintage photograph?

I write these lines today
with love on their behalf.

Be Swift to Love

Don't tell me that she's gone.
I saw her yesterday.
She never said a word
about her plans to go away.

I saw her in the morning
at a table set for one
reflecting on the dreams her mind
the night before had spun.
The house is hers at breakfast.
Her waking wants are few:
a coffee cup and saucer,
a napkin creased in two.
The radio for company,
she banters with a talk show host
until her cup contains
a teaspoonful at most.

She lifts the china to her lips.
The tilted sip exposes
the pattern in the porcelain
of red and yellow roses.
She savors every single drop
concluding her repast
with the frugal luxury
of making good things last.

I saw her in the afternoon
with sheets and pillow cases hung
to billow in the breeze upon
a line from porch to pine tree strung.
She contemplates her handiwork.
The sun is warm upon her skin.

In her imagination
she reels the outdoors in.

I saw her at the end of day
Atlantic breezes in her hair.
While others pack and hurry home
she lingers in a folding chair.
Sandpipers race across the sand
to perch upon a mirrored sky.
She welcomes all within her gaze,
the harvest of a quiet eye.

Don't tell me that she's gone
Her wisdom comes to mind
Be swift to love, she wrote,
make haste to be kind.
Indelible, upon a card,
her cursive hand, her ballpoint ink
an after-dinner lesson
taped above the kitchen sink.
First learned by heart
remembered with a sigh:
one washes while the other dries.

The Milkweed Pod

It wasn't easy to be our mother:
valedictorian, college grad
when women with degrees were rare,
independent, sociable
on track to a career
she set aside for married life.
Last-born, the youngest child
among five siblings,
unprepared for seven of her own,
under chronic stress
in need of comfort and support
not in her nature to request
nor in her husband's to express.
In the end, she did her best.

Years later, we siblings circled back
revisiting a passing we had missed.
Absorbed by families of our own
we failed to see the chasm opening
between her life and ours
until she'd gone beyond
the reach of reminiscence.
More's the pity. It would have gladdened her
to know we'd witnessed her refreshed
in a minute of transcendence.

For summer day-trips
she'd pack a wicker basket
fill a cooler and fold beach towels
while Dad would cinch the folding chairs
to the station wagon roof and drive,
the triple rows of seats fully occupied
for a day of rest and leisure

shaded by a woods around a field,
a marsh, and modest lake.

After hot dogs roasted on a grille,
after celery and carrot sticks,
after dollar bills dispensed
for clinking soda bottles
from the snack bar cooler,
after children banished
to the swings, a slide, a sandy beach,
she'd change into a floral patterned swimsuit
step out of sandals
adjust her bathing cap,
splash calves and wrists,
bend at the waist and glide,
alternating strokes—breast, crawl, side—
until she touched the raft,
caught her breath and pushed away,
back arched, eyes closed,
face shining in the sun.
From the shore
we children paused
to note her transformation,
her true identity revealed
uplifted by the waters
of a deep humanity.

In her final week in hospice care
we should have recognized the swimmer
mixing up her strokes, going further out,
treading water and turning back
until the day no one could save
the tiny figure whose parting wave
tipped her off the edge
of her horizon.

Because we missed
the moment of her passing
our mourning was a lake
too deep for us to touch the bottom
until her wisdom came
arising from the depths
in words that seemed to say:

The dying often pull away
preferring in the end
the intimacy of death
to mortal company.
Like a child who knows the way
like breaking free to fly
like silk that splits a milkweed pod,
their final act, to die, is done
in a private audience with God.

Four:
Good as grass, a gentle state of mind

Prairie Fire

My friend's garage went up in flames
draped the air with inky smoke.
He'd closed the door to manage dust
while stripping ancient varnish
from a maple desk.
Lost in the lustrous grain,
absorbed, at peace, alone,
forgetting solvent fumes
would make a loaded cannon of his craft,
he flipped a switch.
A spark no bigger than a stitch
set off an orange whoosh,
knocked him off his feet
set his clothes on fire and blew the windows out.
The firefighters found my friend inside.
He lingered for a month before he died.

His name was Ron,
park district counselor
in our prairie town.
Gangly, a cornstalk of a man
a connoisseur of riddles
quick to laugh,
slow to speak his mind
but not afraid to disagree.
Attended niece and nephew orchestra recitals
walked his aging neighbor's dog
vacationed with his relatives
cleaned the fish they caught,
carried wood and lit the fire
connected stars, paused to hear
the rustling on the forest floor.

They called him Uncle Ron,
good as grass, a gentle state of mind.
On his watch, no child
was ever lost or left behind.

At the visitation
friends and neighbors
kneeled at coffin side,
said prayers,
bid brief farewells
not wanting to appear to scrutinize
the dead for scars
hidden by a navy suit,
folded hands, and undertaker's art.

We reminisced in lowered voices
poring over photographs on poster boards.
Even as a boy he seemed at ease alone,
behind the candles on a birthday cake
straddling a bicycle, one foot on a pedal,
sprawled across a station wagon tailgate.
Reducing us to whispers,
images of Ron became a leaden collar
tight about our throats.

A good man squandered,
taken in a thoughtless moment
random as a lightning bolt
that sparks a prairie fire,
incinerating nests,
torching dens and burrows,
herding predator and prey
in frantic roundabout.

The smoke would linger
in my mind for years
until I found a clearing
in the thickets of my grief,
as if Ron had called me in
to hear amid the stirring grass
his laughter at my blindness
to a hundred shades of green.

His charred earth healed,
his coffin softened into bedding
for clandestine deer,
his funeral wreaths rebloomed
with shooting stars, coneflower,
wild indigo, their prairie roots
profusely intertwined.

I should have known.
On his watch no child was ever
lost or left behind.

The Groundskeeper

Bill, thick and heavy set
hands like paws
as if built for bearing down
the cemetery grounds,
repairs the headstones
cracked by Appalachian
freeze and thaw.
His walk-behind lawnmower
thrusts out an alligator snout
devised for trimming grass
between the graves too close
to let a standard mower pass.

In a t-shirt stained and worn,
he isn't paid and doesn't ask to be
but pleased to pause for visitors
in search of ancestry.

Bill recognized the names
we'd come to find,
a gnarly limb
branching from our family tree.
He walked us to their plot
waited as we visited
our ancestors at rest
beneath their leaning slabs
in company of lesser stones
an inch above the sod.
Their letters weathered off
spoke of children lost
in the secret words of God.

In a plot nearby
Bill paused to pay respects
before his brother's stone.
Died young, he said.
A quick end in a wreck.

As if the crash were yesterday,
he recalled the undertaker's tact:
An open casket
asks of us a little more.
His mother shook her head,
set upon the coffin lid
a high school photograph:
long-haired, a favorite son,
the life of any party in the county
a crazy grin that seemed to say
life is for the young.

We stood by Bill
twisting at his gloves
remembering his mother's words:
The photograph you hate
so much you learn to love.

The Colors of Home

Welcomed into Nancy's home,
stocked with books and magazines
like platters at a feast
where conversations flow
with acumen and anecdote.

Her paintings speak in languages
of tawny, crimson, blue.
Her husband Harry's memory
remains in amber, marble, stone
sculpted messages to her
of tenderness
inhabiting their home.

Visitors drawn in like me
are kindled by their flame
departing hours later
better than we came.

Parked in the Sixties

How could I have been so naive
too self-absorbed to pray for murdered nurses
hardly hearing shots of a clock tower sniper
believing in the Saigon thugs we called allies?
But I was 15
books and papers spilling from my locker
legs locking up at track meet finish lines
mouthing words of Beatles songs.

How could I have been so shallow
averting eyes from napalmed villages
not showing up at protest rallies
unappalled by race riots broadcast live?
But I was 16
parading behind a pep rally float
sharpening number two pencils for entrance exams
trembling, phone in hand, a girl's voice in my ear.

How could I have been so vain
not sick with grief over Martin and Bobby slain
not sobered by black-gloved fists on Olympic gold
not fearing for classmates bound for war?
but I was 17
a yearbook under my arm
car keys in my pocket,
a tassel looped on the rear view mirror.

Before the soul is plowed,
before amazing friends blend into the crowd,
before the innocence goes,
God must take snapshots
to laugh at with us later.
Why else make the Sixties so over the top
like cruising all night in a blue Dodge Dart
slowing to park
soft clicks of the engine cooling
bench seat adrift in a sea of cars
the windshield a mirror of stars?

Most Wanted

When school vacation afternoons began to drag,
when Moms fed up with squabbles
shooed the kids outdoors,
when no one came to chose up sides,
build a fort, or swap their baseball cards,
when we'd tire of pumping on our pedals,
slamming on the brakes, and leaving skid-mark
curlicues behind,
we'd mount the post office steps
tap the burnished railings
swing the doors by brass handles
cross the polished floor
spin the locks of PO boxes
test the scales and scribble
with ballpoint pens on beaded chains
until most wanted posters stared back at us,
while we inspected faces we might recognize.

Silenced by the thud of hand-stamped cancellations
we mouthed the words
armed robbery, capital murder,
unlawful flight, armed and dangerous.
We'd memorize the grainy black and whites,
the faces flat and dark as manhole covers.
We'd make up true crime stories of our own
mimicking Joe Friday's monotone.

Arrested by imagination
stuck in solitary
most wanted losers
waiting on death row
cursing out a final meal,
the chair, the straps
the switch a hand would throw.

But what did we know?
We were kids in the 1950s
when even though
we couldn't hear we knew
at five o'clock
that mothers up and down the street
stood in open doors
picturing our faces
most wanted innocents
at dinner table places.

Fledgling

The last time I held my niece
half girl, half bird,
perching on my knee,
in a flash I understood,
my mind not wanting to,
why a girl would gain
protective weight
what she'd have to pay to soar
why she'd hide her wings
lest they be broken
by the world outside her door.

A Brush With Madness Starts My Day

I pedaled off from home today,
briefcase bungeed to my luggage rack.
On side streets lined with budding trees
I reveled in my liberty as if the dawn
had scattered gold that might be found
on bicycles, train-station bound.

I could drive the mile or so, but why?
To take five minutes off the trip?
To rumble in a two-ton padded cell
when I could foil friction
on a frame of metal bones,
hollow as a bird's, set upon a pair
of wheels contrived for flight
on tubes of pumped-up air.

I spun the pedals one last time,
the parking rack in sight,
a slot awaiting my front tire,
until, crashing through my reverie,
a man on foot stepped in the way.

I swerved, squeezed on the brakes in time.
Frozen, we looked each other up and down.
I in shirt and tie, he in coat too heavy
for the April air, its long skirts frayed,
a worn felt hat, unshaven face
yet standing tall, unbent by age
a handsome man in better days.

"I object to your bicycle," was all he said,
with dignity as if in court.
Instead of epithet or harsh rebuke,
he lodged his just objection,
addressing not the rider but the bike
before he turned and walked away.

I watched him go
until the clanging crossing bells
hurried me aboard. From a window seat
I searched the station parking lot
but saw no more of him.
Still, I could not help but wonder
where he'd go to be of use,
what purpose might direct his day,
this patron of pedestrians
protesting objects getting in the way.

The Jedi Left Behind

Wincing, I lift a foot to find
a plastic figure, Obi Wan,
a saber-bearing Jedi
our grandsons left behind.

All weekend, their character collection
marched across our kitchen floor,
endangering unslippered feet
like stones unshaken from a shoe,
or like a minefield made of toys
not fatal but best tiptoed through.

Now packed to go, their armies
stowed in bulging carry-alls
set by the door, they pause
for hugs, the boys assigned
to tracking down the mittens,
shoes and socks no one can find.

Our reign restored
the occupying forces gone
all but this straggler
a hero of galactic wars
silent, dark, and vigilant,
set upon the mantlepiece
while grandsons buckled in
are rolling home fast asleep.

The Jedi waits
in service to our heirs,
our lives a prequel
the world becoming theirs:
the toys, the van,
the road, the stars,
a legend of their own.
Only the smart of a stepped on toy
is ours and ours alone.

Explaining Cancer to a Child

Cancer is like going to a monster party. At the end we all take off our costumes and everyone laughs when they see who we really are.

Cancer is like a train wreck. Our years fold upon each other like box cars off the tracks, and best friends lead us to the exits.

Cancer is like the job no one wants but turns out to be the only job that really matters.

Cancer is like a broken heart. It hurts but doesn't punish, and we want the pain to end until it does.

Cancer is like two good things at once—a God who's coming and a God who's already here.

Cancer is like a prayer spoken on God's knee.

Give me only your love and your grace.
That is enough for me.

Stem Cell Transplant

You would have died
if not for her
half a world away.
Asked to join
a donor registry
she said yes.

The treatment plan
had no guarantee
except a year of misery.
Asked to bear
the cruel uncertainty,
you said yes.

Against the odds,
her protein markers
matched yours.
Asked to give
but never know to whom
she said yes.

The pre-transplant
conditioning
ravished your immunities.
Asked to fight
without defenses
you said yes.

The doctors harvested
the stem cells
from her blood.
Asked to be
your stem cell nursery
she said yes.

Your body tagged
her transfused cells
as foreigners.
Asked to brave
rejection risk,
you said yes.

She wondered
if her cells would take.
Although no one could say
if it would help
for her to pray
she said yes.

Emaciated,
dosages reduced,
you seized your life.
Asked to rise, to lift
your legs and walk,
you said yes.

Could lives combine?
Could two be one
that one might suffer less?
Two women
half a world apart,
said yes.

Five:
Forgive me if your name wriggles free

Muscle Memory

Here I come on a bicycle
a man on a wire, precarious me,
impossibly balanced on two skinny tires
unafraid of a nasty fall.
Not once do I wonder how I can still ride.
My muscles remember it all.

Like floating on water, arching your back
eyes looking up, shoulders relaxed
like making your way in an unlit room
in a house where you've lived before
you find your way by touch—
less by mind and more
by comprehension of the limbs and core.

You are young as the things your muscles recall—
how to pucker your lips to whistle
how to ramble, meander, and roam
and once you've left your nest behind
how to make the road your home.

You are young as the things you can never unfeel—
to love and be loved in return
to greet an old friend after too many years
to forgive your mistakes and learn
to know when it's time to put down a dog
whose eyes still follow you everywhere,
how to lift your eyes to the hills with thanks
for the stone in the shoe you wear.

You are young as the ways
you learn to let go—
how to set your mind aside and bow
to what your muscles know
and once you've gone as far as you can
how to turn around and pedal home.

Lost Keys

Forgive me if your name
wriggles free, slippery and silver,
from my aging memory.
Be patient, please
until I crack the mystery
of where I left my keys.

The experts say
these awkward episodes
arise from inattention,
not forgetfulness.
With mind on mid-day meds
braking for a shopping list
bumpered by a book that's overdue
cut off by wedding gifts to buy and send,
pulled over by a diagnostic test, flashers on,
my power of recall
is a rush-hour traffic jam
slowing to a crawl.

Bear with me in this bottleneck.
I'll soon be getting through.
Your name will come to mind.
The keys will reappear as if on cue
while elsewhere in my memory
beloved faces old and new
my dearest inventory,
rock gently, close to shore,
tethered to the mooring buoys
of my remembered story.

The Night-light

When entering a darkened room
who hasn't felt the border melt
between the past and present tense,
between the here and someplace else?

You know how it is to feel for a switch
and come up wall. You grope, aghast.
The switch you sought and missed retreats
as if your hand had reached into the past.

Transported by your startled fingertips,
you visit places, knowing they are gone
yet coming into view before the flip
of felt-for switch has turned the lights back on.

In this past restored a night-light glows.
Familiar bedtime stories fill a shelf.
The mound beneath the covers is the child
you were, attended by a future self.

The Beach

There is a solitary beach
above the waterline of sleep
where memories lie on their sides
unlifted by the highest tides.

Little here might cause a gull to screech,
pivot on the wind and weightlessly alight
to take a left-eyed look with head turned right.
Nor would the barefoot crowds
care to comb the wreckage of regret.
Their souvenirs are gathered wet—
shells and skipping stones
not photographs of loved ones lost
whose silhouettes remain
in a driftwood picture frame.

Not in a bed but on this beach
I lie tonight, not blessed to know
the gracious ocean's ebb and flow.
Beyond the breakers' furthest reach
untouched by fingertips of wind-blown spray
or goddesses arising from the foam,
nothing on this beach is washed away
or by the currents carried home.

The Mentalist's Lament

There are benefits, I would agree
to having photographic memory
but still, before you envy me
appreciate the storage in your mind.

You have a gallery of portraits
conversing with each other and your present self.
The oil paints of still lifes show
the things you once confused with wealth,
while watercolor landscapes recreate
the places you have been
and would extend your stay
to browse the folios of sketches not yet on display.

Your memories contain more metaphor than fact.
Their sequence and perspective shift
defying intellectual review,
and yet these illustrations fit you like a second skin
colored by the many ways of being true—
a place where you may bid
another in to share your point of view.

As for me, I have a database
catalogued by what and when.
I can tell you where I've been
by day and date from an early age.
The people I have met—every last one of them—
I can reel them off ad infinitum.

Lucky me, exposed by my photography
from now to when my memories begin,
but what I wouldn't give to have a single page
like yours to frame my story in.

Weekend Update

Four single friends, three bedrooms
plus a sofa, first jobs out of college,
weekdays working late, weekends
pouring wine for someone else's guest,
when parties didn't start before 11,
when improv on TV was new,
when we were wild and crazy guys,
re-enacting skits we'd memorized.
Where the party went from there God only knew.

Laughter then was Cherry Coke
a sugar rush of comic bits
shaken, fizzing up
a running over cup of greatest hits.

Now in independent living
awaiting dinner served at four,
ancient boomers watch old episodes
of SNL, our laughter thickened into caramel
sea-salted by comedians
on the scene when we were young,
Weekend Update anchors half a century ago.

As if the party never stopped
I fill a glass of wine for someone new.
How she knows my name I couldn't say
but she just made me laugh.
No one can make us stop.
Don't even try.

That's how it feels to be alive
when we are younger than our fears.
That's how it felt to laugh, minus 50 years.

Six:
Follow the sound of singing

Good Friday

If by loving the gentle among us, we become gentle
if by faith in fragile things, we become fragile
if we succumb with the easily crushed
we graciously oblige.

Compassion proven wrong
a thousand times and yet
we love the poorest of the poor.
Warned to shun their needy touch
we ache from wanting more.

If broken into smithereens
fragile things assemble
secured by silken strands
of a web of faith
spun by unseen hands.

Though crushed beneath
the boot of the world
we press on, coalescing
like beads of oil,
oozing forth a blessing.

Listen. Follow the sound of singing.
If we are late, wait for us.
Lift up your eyes.
We the gentle, the fragile, the easily crushed
will rise.

So Big

Poetry is big enough for mass shootings
blood diamonds and suicide vests,
big enough for toxic spills,
birth defects and Amazon burning,
big enough for genocide,
opioids and species extinction,
big enough for border walls,
refugee camps and pandemics,
big enough for dirty tricks
hush money and hate crimes,
big enough for child soldiers
IEDs and slavery,
and still has room for oxygen,
manatees, arctic terns
hummingbirds, coral reefs
grand slams, perfect games
rose windows, libraries
northern lights, redwood trees
vineyards, luaus
bicycles, chocolate bars
cascades and cherry blossoms
along with courage, truth and hope
the promise of humanity
which is to say
never, never, never underestimate
the bounds of poetry.

The Thing With Feathers

On the worst of the worst of awful days
consider the expanding universe
bulging out with more than enough
horrid and gorgeous stuff.

As smooth as a whale scoops sardines,
the world makes room for mass shootings
child soldiers and ebola outbreaks.

As quick as an eel in a heron's beak,
the dark abyss gives way to opioids
lead paint chips and rigged elections.

As deft as an otter cracking a clam,
a hidden door slides back on cover-ups
forest fires and species extinction.

All the unremitting gruesome stuff
keeps grinding away until we're left
with heartless, hopeless sacks of rubble
that can't be given or taken back.

On such a day, when the reasonable thing to do
is stay in bed, expect the worst, and whimper
an existential, candle-snuffing toast
to a world in total disarray,
what made the guy ahead of you
in the drive-through lane
pay your check and drive away?

Ode to a Sneeze

When I go, let it be
not with a weary dying wheeze
but with the gusto of a sneeze,

a sneeze to shake me free
from remnants of mortality,
a hearty send-off for my passage
toward eternity,

and when my decongested soul
nears its everlasting goal
let God's clear voice be heard to say
Gesundheit, friend, please come this way.

Georgia Peaches

Twice a summer
before the Midwest county fairs
have come and gone,
a refrigerated semi
exits off the interstate.
It rumbles to a stop
on the Tractor Supply
store blacktop
where we stand and wait
for Georgia peaches.

Our Prairie State
grows corn and beans with ease.
The farmers' market carts
are overstocked
with radishes,
green peppers,
summer squash,
tomatoes, cukes,
fruits and berries
of the season.
Not peaches, though.
Peaches need a warmer zone
with milder winters
and summers sultry
as a small-town floozy
flirting, juiced, the chef and she
in an all-night diner booth.

Back at the truck
our neighbors seem to hold their breath
imagining cobblers, crisps, and crumbles,
preserves in mason jars,
braided coffee cakes
from heirloom recipes

sweeter than the deadly sins
or unadorned
hand-held, eaten whole,
sweet juices running down
our fingers, lips, and chins.

A crew of good old boys
swings wide the trailer doors,
bantering with customers
unloading sturdy cardboard boxes
half a bushel each
onto battered tables,
a folding shrine for taking orders
from the next in line.
Stacks of cash multiply
so fast it almost fools the eye
to see the 10s and 20s
reappear in rubber-banded rolls
bulging out the pockets
of the cashier's overalls.

By sunset in kitchens
all around the town
peaches commandeer
the horizontal surfaces
from countertops to pantry shelves.
Straight from the box,
a Georgia peach is firm
unyielding to the touch
as green tomatoes
until in several days or so
when a thumb-press
leaves an imprint,
when crow's-feet wrinkles
show around the stem,

when rosy blush gives way
to a rush of yellow gold
then we know we've waited long enough
for Georgia peaches to rise to lusciousness.

The first bite breaks the skin
tissue thin, unresisting,
the juicy sweetness
exploding on the tongue.
We almost moan,
each bite made sweeter
to the taste and eye
by ruby streaks
bleeding from the stone.

Only then do we remember
half a bushel ripened all at once
is a plethora for two.
If left unturned a peach's heft
will tenderize the underside.
We move them to the fridge
but there's no stopping peaches
once they start to go.
You'd think by now we'd know
how many are enough
but queued up in the parking lot,
all we have in mind is peach perfection
quashing any thought of having far too much.

Nothing we can do but share
our ripened trove with neighbors
pleased to take as much as we can spare.
This is no ordinary harvest,

no surplus of tomato vines
and pepper plants from backyard plots
whose keepers give away as much as anyone will take
and still have excess on their hands.
No, each and every peach is in demand
shared and savored
as if it had a voice to say:

Goodness, real goodness, comes like Georgia peaches
it can't be staged or slowed
or otherwise delayed.
Real goodness won't be planned.
It ripens all at once, so sticky sweet
it makes us lick the juices off our hands.

When goodness comes, nothing is
or could be half as good
as urgently desired
as produce from a serpent's tree
as if a twig transported
surreptitiously from Eden
were grafted to a mortal stock
to yield a peach, a crop,
as tempting and delicious
as any other earthly sweet
that dangles out of reach.

When goodness comes,
it comes by truckloads on a summer afternoon.
It overruns the courthouse square,
the churches, fences,
monuments and cemeteries
in a rising tide. It picks up speed
in need of nothing more to be complete
until we know there is no sin but one—

to let a single peach be wasted
to never touch a human tongue
for God to make this world, His peach,
and let it go untasted.

Grace

Even after I'd spoiled everything
had lost my way and self-respect
you wouldn't slight or love me less,
which proves that fallen apples have their place
with those untouched by sod
when crushed by time and love and grace
in the cider press of God.

The Crooked Path

The sad, sad morning after,
after the looting, the overturned cars,
the burned out stores,
after the forest fire of rage,
when shopkeepers return
to wreckage of dreams
to all the ugliness that comes
from holding a man face down
to the pavement, a knee to his neck.

How can anyone blame men so abused
for jumping at a chance to get even,
if only a few night's fury?
How can anyone think it's enough
to protect what we have
while those with so little have lost so much?

The ending may be even sadder.
The rage will burn out,
the looters driven off,
the protestors heading home
until the desperate few are left behind,
the ones with nothing left to lose
who will be rounded up, tried, and put away
unless in years to come,
a people pushed too far may be remembered
trudging on mankind's crooked path
toward a more just world.

Is This How Meeting God Will Be?

After the heat of the day
after the last pitch
after the players clear the field,
we rise to join the slow-moving crowd
dazed from a day in the sun
shuffling through the concourse
pennants limp from waving
programs left behind,
no matter who cheered or booed
or caught a foul
or won or lost.

What matters is the God
who gave us tickets and said
Look for me after the game.
We forgot of course,
swept up in baseball's fever
the meteor streak to the plate
the infield hops, the pick-off plays
the arms like cannons
firing from the outfield
their shells exploding at home,
until the sun-baked ushers
coaxed us toward the gates
which was where we saw Him
seeing us first
tipping His cap
the game ball in His glove.

Is this what He meant
by a God whose play
is to catch us by surprise
waving us in
at the end of game
right before our eyes?

Never Ordinary

I have never gone to war, stormed a beach
or led a charge of fearless men,
but I have been an idiot with women
who loved me anyway.

I have never fought a duel, dodged a bullet
or played the most dangerous game,
but I have learned to bathe a dog
and not get sopped in spray.

I have never sworn to bloodied brothers
that history will know our name,
but I have pedaled past an outraged dog
and been the one who got away.

I have never survived a stroke
or run when no one thought I'd walk again,
but I have been a child's soft place to fall
on broken-hearted days.

I have never struck it rich, lost a fortune
or sold my soul at the devil's door,
but I have witnessed human light
defy the night with gentle glory.

I have never blazed a trail, stared down a bear
or gone where no man went before,
but I have learned to love the ordinary
as much as a good story
if not a little more.

About the Author

Kevin Shyne is a lifelong writer whose career included 12 years as a freelance magazine writer and 23 years as a corporate speechwriter. Active in creative writing since high school, he took a deeper dive into poetry after his retirement in 2013.

Kevin and his wife, Debi, raised their two daughters in the Chicago suburbs before moving to Princeton, a small town in the corn-and-soybean heart of North Central Illinois.

Kevin is active in the Illinois River Valley poetry community, taking part in poetry readings and critique workshops. In 2018, Kevin and a small group of volunteers organized The Festival of the Written Word, a one-day celebration of creative writing for students at eight high schools in Bureau County, Illinois.

Kevin writes poetry to cope with grief and defeat, to celebrate love and redemption, and to reflect on the beauty of ordinary living. His poems have been published in numerous journals and have been recognized in poetry competitions sponsored by the Niles (Illinois) Public Library and *The Bureau County Republican* newspaper.